101 LESSONS

THEY NEVER TAUGHT YOU IN HIGH SCHOOL ABOUT GOING TO COLLEGE

PRACTICAL ADVICE FOR HIGH SCHOOLERS
CROWDSOURCED FROM COLLEGE STUDENTS
AND RECENT GRADUATES

MARK BEAL

D1115729

Published by Mark Beal Media, LLC
Toms River, New Jersey

Cover Design: Evan Carroll

ISBN: 978-1986410083

First Printing: 2018 Printed in the United States of America

101 Lessons They Never Taught You In High School About Going To College is available for bulk orders, special promotions and premiums. For details, call +1.848.992.0391 or email markbeal@markbealmedia.com.

This book is dedicated to the more than 1,000 university students I have taught and mentored since 2013. They have inspired me to continuously learn, evolve and transform.

ACKNOWLEDGEMENTS

In 2013, I started teaching in the School of Communication at Rutgers University. Since that time, I have taught and mentored more than 1,000 college students as they prepare for the transition from college to a career. It was the many questions from these students about their preparation for their future careers that inspired me to author *101 Lessons They Never Taught You In College* in 2017. As the book received praise from media and college students nationwide, I realized that these same college students could be a great resource for the next generation of college students, today's high schoolers. So, I set out on a journey to write *101 Lessons They Never Taught You In High School About Going To College.*

I first want to thank all the current college students and recent graduates who responded to my inquiry for a lesson they would share with high schoolers about making the transition to college. More than 40 individuals representing more than 15 universities nationwide submitted at least one lesson and they include Meghan Beal (Kean University), Summer Beal (East Stroudsburg University), Jesse Ruela (Penn State University), Antonia Attardo (Rutgers University), Avery McWilliams (Rutgers University), Austin Sommerer (Penn State University), Meryl Parseghian (Rutgers University), Caroline Petrone (University of South Carolina), Melissa Jannuzzi (Rutgers University), Reid Burch (Loyola University Maryland) Andrew Davis (Rutgers University), Lexi Amato (Emerson College), Zahra Abbasi (Rutgers University), Sierra Haney (The College of New Jersey), Carly Galasso (Rutgers University), Carly Wilhelm (Northeastern University), Alec Prieto (Rutgers University), Emma Sinanan (Pace University), Kelsey Cuje (Rutgers University), Rachel Boyce (Stockton University), Pat Kelly (Rutgers University), Alyssa Dell'Acqua (Charleston Southern

University), Ashley DeSalvatore (Rutgers University), Noel Fratto (Johnson & Wales University), Stephen Moodie (Rutgers University), Kate Galgano (The College of New Jersey), Ryan Rose (Rutgers University), Paige Daly (University of New Haven), Ryan Diminick (Rutgers University), Jacqueline Manza (Northwestern State University), Ari Gutman (Rutgers University), Dana Carbone (Monmouth University), Troy Anthony (Rutgers University), Grace Boyd-Dias (Rutgers University), Jenifer Elizondo (Rutgers University), Samantha Franco (Rutgers University), Rebecca Shapiro (Rutgers University), Kimberly Jones (Rutgers University), Daijie Yuan (Rutgers University), Kasey Chan (Rutgers University) and Gedalya Gerstle (Rutgers University).

I would like to thank my wife, Michele. Thank you for all the time you allow me to pursue my passion projects and challenge my creative and strategic mind. It's only due to the many sacrifices you have made over the past 30 years that I have been able to evolve and transform as a husband, marketer, educator and author.

I would like to thank our children: Drew and his wife, Huda, who have provided tremendous support to me behind-the-scenes as I pursued this book project; Meghan, who consistently inspires me with creative solutions to the challenges I attempt to solve including this latest book; and Summer, who is a proud member of the East Stroudsburg University class of 2018, and whose graduation not only inspired me to author this book but led to her writing the book's foreword which I am especially proud.

I also have to thank the next generation – my grandsons, Luke and Marc. For the past two years, Luke has inspired me to look at the world in a completely different way and to focus on what is really important in life. While Marc will not attend college for another 18 years, his arrival in this world in 2018 is just the latest blessing in a lifetime full of blessings.

I would like to thank my partners and collaborators in marketing for the past 30 years - Tony Signore, Bryan Harris and John Liporace. Without their inspiration, drive and motivation to always evolve and transform as a professional and human being, I would never had pursued teaching at the university level or authoring books.

I would like to thank Evan Carroll for transforming my thoughts and concepts into a book that high school students across the nation can read as they begin their college career. Thank you for the time and dedication you invested in the book design and layout.

I would like to thank Carly Galasso for reviewing and editing on an ongoing basis as the book evolved.

I would like to thank Stan Phelps, author of the Goldfish series of books and motivational speaker, for always answering my questions regarding authoring a book and many other topics that we have discussed over the past 25 years.

I would like to thank David Dodds for always lending his creative photography expertise to my passion projects, including this book and my previous book.

I would like to thank my colleagues at Rutgers University including Brian Householder, Steve Miller and Jack Grasso and Ken Hunter. If they did not welcome me into their community of higher learning I never would have had the opportunity to be inspired by the brilliance of today's university students.

I would like to thank all of those who volunteer their time to regularly speak to my Rutgers students and provide valuable advice and counsel including Sammy Steinlight, Gordon Deal, Eric Liebler, Keith Green, Jon Landman, Kristina Amaral, Javid Louis, Melissa Jannuzzi and many others.

I would like to thank TJ Pingitore, founder of Student Success U, and his colleague, Sean Molloy, for bringing my 101 Lessons books to life via my 101 Lessons In Leadership podcast series which can be found at www.101lessonspodcast.com

Finally, I would like to thank all the "givers" in my professional and social networks. Your outpouring of support in the form of social media content and word-of-mouth recommendations for my various passion projects including my two books and podcast series transcend what I ever could have imagined. There are far too many of you to list in this book, but my goal is to thank each and every one of you in-person when our paths next meet.

PRAISE FOR 101 LESSONS THEY NEVER TAUGHT YOU IN HIGH SCHOOL ABOUT GOING TO COLLEGE

"This book is a must read for every student going into college and for every parent who is supporting their child as they embark on their college journey. It will help absorb the shock of that first year in college and make the transition from high school much more effective and enjoyable."

TJ PINGITORE, FOUNDER, STUDENT SUCCESS U

"There is no greater way for an incoming freshman to gain practical knowledge about attending college than reading the lessons taught in this book."

CHRISTOPHER BEAL, ASSISTANT PRINCIPAL, SALESIAN HIGH SCHOOL

"This book is filled with the type of advice I give my own teen daughters on how to prepare for and succeed in college. Many high school students eagerly anticipate heading off to school, yet don't know what they're about to experience, or how to cope. Mark Beal's book helps make this clear."

KEN HUNTER, ADJUNCT PROFESSOR, RUTGERS UNIVERSITY

"As someone who has worked on college campuses for more than 25 years, I guarantee that any student who follows the advice presented in this book will have an extremely rewarding and successful college career. Those who read it will maximize their experience over the next four years and beyond."

JOE LYNCH, EXECUTIVE DIRECTOR OF ALUMNI RELATIONS, GETTYSBURG COLLEGE

"It's no exaggeration that this book will motivate any freshman. Mark Beal intertwines personal advice from current college students and graduates. These lessons are crucial for success in college."

KELSEY CUJE, RUTGERS UNIVERSITY, CLASS OF 2017

"My younger brother is graduating high school and entering his first year as a college student. With 101 Lessons They Never Taught You In High School About Going To College being published this spring, I now have the perfect graduation gift to give him."

MELISSA JANNUZZI, RUTGERS UNIVERSITY, CLASS OF 2017

"College was one of the most positive and transformative periods of my life. If I had this incredible tool available to me at that time, it would have been like adding rocket fuel to my college experience."

MATT VAN TUINEN, MARKETING COMMUNICATIONS AGENCY, CEO

"As a recent college graduate, I can attest to how valuable a resource this book is for all incoming freshman. The access to lessons developed through recent real-world university experiences makes this required reading for any student looking to get the most out of their journey through college."

RYAN ROSE, RUTGERS UNIVERSITY, CLASS OF 2017

"At any stage, a tireless work ethic joined by a capable skill set, (sprinkled with "Lady Luck"), only evens the odds on one's journey to career fulfillment. The practical lessons delivered by Mark Beal in this must-read will more clearly distinguish an incoming collegian's search for defined clarity...and continued success."

SAMMY STEINLIGHT, PUBLIC RELATIONS AGENCY, CEO

TABLE OF CONTENTS

PART I: FAMILY & FRIENDS

PART II: CLASSES & PROFESSORS

PART III: IT'S ALL ABOUT YOU

PART IV: LOOKING AHEAD TO YOUR CAREER

PART V: PHILOSOPHY 101

FOREWORD

BY SUMMER BEAL

As I was completing my senior year of college at East Stroudsburg University as a proud member of the Class of 2018, I was beyond thrilled when my dad asked if I would have the honor of writing the foreword to his latest book, *101 Lessons They Never Taught You In High School About Going To College*. If I had this book at the beginning of my college career, the transition from high school to college would have been far less complicated and much more seamless, as my dad crowdsourced tips and advice from current college students as well as recent graduates, including many of his Rutgers University students.

In the final lesson of his first book, *101 Lessons They Never Taught You In College*, my dad encourages college students and recent graduates to "Be A Student For Life." That very important lesson could easily be the first lesson in this new book which offers high school graduates a roadmap to success in college based on the experiences of more than 40 college students and recent graduates nationwide.

For any recent high school graduate who is preparing to go to college, one of the greatest resources you will have will be an army of professors, counselors and advisors. I wish before I started college that someone had shared with me Lesson #14: Use Your Professors...They Want You To. If I knew this earlier in my college career, my start would have been much stronger and smarter. More often than not, your professors and other campus advisors will be available to meet regularly outside the classroom. With that tuition bill, comes your right to request assistance and leverage valuable on-campus resources. Those resources should be leveraged now as you take your first college courses and in the future as you plan the transition from college to a career. Additionally, the earlier you begin networking with your professors and advisors, the more likely they will be inclined later in your college career to write a letter of recommendation on your behalf for an internship, job or acceptance into a master's program.

College is all about becoming who you want to be. Part III of this book includes critical lessons that will help you evolve and reach your greatest potential before graduation. Lesson #42: Be Proud of You, sounds very simple, but it's something that can easily be forgotten. Each and every day of your college experience presents an opportunity for you to excel. By the end of the day or week when you finish your last class, you want to be able to look in the mirror and know you have challenged yourself and you have left nothing on the table. By being confident in your approach and empowering yourself to experience the endless opportunities college has to offer, you will have transformed yourself by the time you graduate, eager and excited for everything the world has to offer you.

Finally, no matter how incredible your college experience is, never forget Lesson #1: You Can Go Home. College is a time in your life when you get to discover yourself without mom and dad holding your hand, but never forget where you came from. Your parents are your biggest cheerleaders. They want to see you succeed as much as you do... if not more. Without the help of my parents, Michele and Mark Beal, I would not be the woman I am today, prepared, excited and ready to take on every challenge that comes my way after graduation. While my love of marketing came from my dad, both my parents instilled in me the drive to succeed, the confidence to challenge the status quo and the ability to recognize and celebrate every accomplishment no matter how big or small.

Whether you are attending community college down the street from your home or moving cross-country to a major university, the lessons in this book, which were inspired by those college students who once were freshman just like you, will inform, inspire, motivate and challenge you as you start one of the most exciting chapters in your life. Good luck and best wishes for great success on your incredible journey through college!

INTRODUCTION

Imagine, you just completed high school, and more than 40 college students or recent graduates from more than 15 universities nationwide hand you a playbook that will set you up for success as you are about to step foot on campus for the next four years. Well, that is exactly what this book, *101 Lessons They Never Taught You In High School About Going To College*, is intended to do.

Having taught in the School of Communication at Rutgers University since 2013, I have been inspired by the more than 1,000 university students I have had the privilege to teach. After authoring my first book in 2017, *101 Lessons They Never taught You In College*, which was intended to help my students make the transition to a career, I thought that my current students and recent graduates could offer advice and lessons to the next generation of college students.

If I was a high school senior preparing to go to college I could not imagine a better resource for advice than current college students and recent graduates. The 101 lessons in this book were inspired by students at universities and colleges across the nation who are currently immersed in the college experience or recently completed their time on campus. The 101 lessons they inspired are unprecedented and provide a roadmap for freshman as they navigate their new world as students of higher learning. To the college students who contributed to this book, I thank you very much. To those just beginning their journey through college, I wish you nothing but tremendous success and an experience that is more than you could have ever imagined that will serve as a solid foundation for your future.

As you spend your summer preparing for college, please thumb through this book. It was written and designed in a way that you can randomly open to any page or lesson and gain valuable insights that you can apply the first day you step on campus. I would recommend that you keep this book in your backpack and pull it out and reference when you are facing a new challenge and seeking a solution.

PART I

FAMILY & FRIENDS

LESSON 1

YOU CAN GO HOME

Contributed by Summer Beal,
East Stroudsburg University, Class of 2018

Contrary to many people who may advise you that when you leave for college never look back, always remember that you have a tremendous support system back home. Attending college does not have to be a choice between campus and home. You can enjoy the best of both worlds throughout your college years. Aside from your home being a physical destination where you can recharge your batteries, enjoy mom's cooking and get a quality night's sleep in your old bedroom, home is where you can seek advice, confide in others about any challenges you may be having at college or just rant about your roommate who never goes to sleep until the sun rises. Consider your home support system a key element of a successful four or five-year college experience. No matter how often you change roommates, professors or close friends throughout your college years, your home will be a consistent base to return, refresh and rethink the challenges before you.

LESSON 2

DON'T FORGET YOUR FAMILY

Contributed by Avery McWilliams,
Rutgers University, Class of 2017

Your family raised you for the first 18 years of your life and you should never forget that now that you have entered your age of independence. No matter how busy you get in college, especially in that first semester, don't forget to update your family and let them know how you are doing. Instead of just sending a series of short text messages, make a phone call or skype at least once a week to share your exciting experiences and daunting challenges. While your family may not be with you on campus, they think about you all the time and would love nothing more than to hear from you and learn all about your new life in college. You don't want to fall into a routine of only calling your family when you need them. You will want to reach out to your family consistently in a way that you maintain an open line of communication and give your family the chance to share in your exciting college experience.

LESSON 3

SHADOW YOUR PARENTS

Contributed by Austin Sommerer,
Penn State University, Class of 2017

From the day you graduate high school until your first moment on campus, shadow your parents, literally. Learn how to wash and dry your clothes, manage your time more effectively and make the most of what little money you may have while taking advantage of promotions, special offers and coupons. Your parents have already earned their PhD in all these areas that will be critical to your way of living, especially in those first few weeks away from home when you are staring at a washing machine for the first time in your life and don't know the difference between the cold and warm rinse, you'll be glad you asked for some help. While you may not want to admit it, your parents can provide incredibly valuable training the summer before you head off to campus especially when it comes to living on your own for the first time.

LESSON 4

OLD FRIENDS, NEW FRIENDS, FUTURE FRIENDS - YOU CAN HAVE THEM ALL

Contributed by Meryl Parseghian,
Rutgers University, Class of 2017

There is no limit to how many people you can meet and interact with while in college. In fact, the more friends, the better. You don't even need to leave your high school friends behind. They can serve as the foundation of your powerful social network that potentially can expand and evolve each and every day throughout college. The key with your network of old, new and future friends is that you should consider all these relationships as mutually beneficial. Everyone in your social network should be someone you can help now or in the future and vice versa. Whether that is assistance with a challenging class or help securing a future internship or job, mobilize your network of friends for good causes and positive results.

Author's Note: As I wrote in my previous book, there is nothing better than being the type of person who is a "giver" and who has friends that do the same.

LESSON 5

BRANCH OUT BEYOND YOUR IMMEDIATE FRIENDS

Contributed by Melissa Jannuzzi,
Rutgers University, Class of 2017

Beyond your high school friends, some of whom may go to the same college, and your roommates, college is the time to branch out and meet as many new people as possible. College should be the opposite of the cliques you may have formed with the tight-knit group of friends you had in high school. Think of college as the first step in developing a professional network that will carry you through your career for the next 30 years. Every individual that you will potentially meet in the classroom, at a club meeting and while playing intramural sports is someone who you may be socially and professionally connected to for the next several decades. Here's a challenge - try to meet and make a meaningful connection with one individual every day starting with your first day on campus. Imagine, meeting 90 new people every semester who could potentially be friends and professional colleagues for life.

LESSON 6

CREATE A CORE GROUP OF FRIENDS

Contributed by Andrew Davis,
Rutgers University, Class of 2017

Throughout college, you will have the opportunity to meet someone new each and every day. You will have friends and classmates come in and out of your college life each semester based on the courses you take, the clubs you join and the places where you live. As you meet new people and make friends, give serious thought to creating a core group of friends or an inner circle of people who challenge each other to grow and evolve. You can easily do this as you start taking courses in your major area of study. As you take the courses required for your major, you will most likely start sitting in class with the same people. As you spend more time with these classmates who share a similar major, align yourself with those who demonstrate ambition and a proactive mindset in the classroom. It is these fellow students who will not only help you evolve while in college, but will also be a critical part of your professional network for many years to come.

LESSON 7

DIVERSIFY YOUR INNER CIRCLE

Contributed by Avery McWilliams,
Rutgers University, Class of 2017

While the previous lesson in this book recommends establishing a core group of friends, it is also very important not to isolate yourself from diverse people and their unique stories. In other words, don't establish such a core group of peers that you ignore many interesting and diverse people who could come into your life each and every day of college. Be open to meeting individuals from different majors, backgrounds and upbringings. By diversifying your circle of friends, you will set a precedent for something that will be very important as you start your career where embracing diversity is a characteristic of a transformative leader.

LESSON 8

MAKE A NEW FRIEND EVERY DAY

Contributed by Zahra Abbasi,
Rutgers University, Class of 2016

Imagine if you made a new friend every single day throughout your college career. It's not as impossible as it sounds. However, it's more of a mindset than an actual goal. Every day when you leave your dorm room or commute to campus, have the mindset that you are going to proactively introduce yourself to others. Instead of walking across campus with your head down and your eyes glue to your mobile phone, look up and into the eyes of those fellow students and professors who you come across. Actually, greet others with a "Good Morning" or "Have A Great Day." You will be pleasantly surprised by the reaction and response you receive. If you go through college with that type of friendly attitude, your experience will be unmatched.

PART II

CLASSES & PROFESSORS

LESSON 9

GO TO CLASS

Contributed by Meryl Parseghian,
Rutgers University, Class of 2017

There is no confusion with this lesson. It is as direct as any in this book. No matter how early in the morning a class takes place or how late on a Thursday night, never skip class. I repeat, never skip class. Skipping class is the easiest thing you can do which is why many students may be tempted to do it. Most professors are more interested in teaching and delivering value to you than simply just taking attendance. Whether your professor takes attendance or not, never miss a class. While skipping may be easy, so is attending class. It really does not take much to walk across campus and attend class for 80 minutes. However, take this lesson one step further. Just don't attend class, be an active participant. By attending every class and participating, you will never fall behind in your course work and you will set yourself up for success in the classroom and well beyond.

LESSON 10

SIT STRATEGICALLY

Contributed by Sierra Haney,
The College of New Jersey, Class of 2018

If you made the effort to get out of bed and trudge your way to the academic building on the outskirts of campus to attend an early morning class, you have already done all the hard work. Now that you are in attendance, be an active participant and sit strategically. There have been plenty of stories written about the science of sitting in a classroom.

Author's Note: From my experience having taught nearly a thousand university students, I take notice of those students who sit front and center consistently. I take even more notice of those students who participate by asking questions and offering commentary. I highly recommend not being a back row bystander or a corner coward. Instead, proactively introduce yourself to the professor, make an immediate connection and carry that connection through the remainder of the semester. The students I have taught who have taken this strategic approach to classroom participation have made a lasting impression with me and are the same students who I am eager to recommend for future internships and jobs or write a strong recommendation letter on their behalf.

LESSON 11

GET AHEAD

Contributed by Caroline Petrone,
University of South Carolina, Class of 2017

Don't delay. Don't procrastinate. Get ahead of all your course work, assignments, projects and preparation for tests and exams. Managing five or more courses each semester requires effective time management and skill at juggling simultaneous deadlines. You will learn quickly that after the first week or two of making introductions in your classes and reviewing the syllabus, college courses take off quickly. First, don't skip any of your classes. The moment you skip a class, you have missed a lecture and most likely an assignment that was explained in detail by the professor. Second, take full advantage of having that syllabus or online class portal where you can actually get ahead of your course work. If you are fortunate to have a professor who designed the entire course online, always look ahead one week ahead to prepare for the next lecture, required reading and assignment. If you can get ahead of your work in each class, you will set yourself up for a successful semester.

LESSON 12

GET OFF TO A STRONG START

Contributed by Carly Galasso,
Rutgers University, Class of 2018

If you speak to any college graduate, the most popular piece of advice or lesson they may offer is to get off to the strongest start possible your freshman year. A very poor first semester or two in the classroom could set you so far back you may be trying to catch up right through graduation day. Imagine, you just left mom and dad's house to live somewhere else for the first time in your life and when you arrive there happen to be a couple of thousand other teenagers in the same situation. The last thing on your mind may be attending class or completing your assignments on time or at a high level. No matter how persuasive your new friends and roommates may be, make a commitment freshman year, or for that matter, every year, to take your classes seriously. If you attend class, you can stay ahead of your assignments and if you stay ahead of your assignments, you will set yourself up for a much stronger start to your college career than one highlighted by absenteeism, missed or late assignments and poor test grades. Your future self will thank you immensely when you get to senior year if you can get off to a strong start freshman year.

LESSON 13

READ THE REVIEWS

Contributed by Meghan Beal,
Kean University, Class of 2014

Before you go out to lunch or dinner or purchase a ticket for a movie, I am sure you take quality time to read the reviews, so why wouldn't you do the same before committing to a 14-week college course? You are going to invest three hours a week listening to a professor and additional hours meeting with the professor during office hours. Don't you want it to be the best possible learning experience it can be? Before registering for a course, take inventory of the various professors assigned to teach. Once you have their names, conduct initial research via *Rate My Professors*. This online discussion board features student reviews of thousands of professors at hundreds of universities across the nation. The commentary and reviews by students should inform you which professor may be the best match for you. Once you have narrowed your list, ask other students if they have had the professor for the same course and learn if there anecdotal feedback reinforces what you learned via *Rate My Professors*. You are not looking for the easiest professor, you are looking for one that will help you evolve and flourish the most throughout the semester.

LESSON 14

USE YOUR PROFESSORS... THEY WANT YOU TO

Contributed by Alec Prieto,
Rutgers University, Class of 2018

No matter how intimidated you may have been by your high school teachers or how anxious you are about your future professors, put your fears aside. I have yet to meet a professor who did not want to help their students as much as possible. You simply need to ask. Editor's Note: Outside the classroom, I have helped hundreds of students revise their resumes, meet individuals in my professional network, secure internships and prepare for job interviews. Each of those collaborative experiences began with a student simply asking for my assistance either after class one day or by sending a one or two sentence email. You should recognize your professors as much more than someone who delivers a lecture or administers a test. Your professors are real people with life experiences and professional relationships that could benefit you significantly if you simply just ask for help.

LESSON 15

BEFRIEND YOUR PROFESSORS

Contributed by Ari Gutman,
Rutgers University, Class of 2017

In your first and second semester on campus, you may be a bit intimidated by your professors. After all, you recently graduated from high school and they are seasoned professors in the school of higher learning. You just have to remind yourself, professors are people too. No matter how intimidated or nervous you may be to befriend your professor, they actually want to help you and see you succeed in and out of the classroom. I have never met a professor who didn't want to assist a student who proactively asked for help. Professors are often asked to serve as references for students when they apply for internships or full-time jobs or to write a letter of recommendation when they apply to graduate school. I highly recommend you strike up a relationship with each of your professors beyond the in-class lectures, assignments and tests by visiting them during office hours, learning more about them while they learn about you and establishing a collaborative relationship that will last a lifetime.

LESSON 16

STUDY IN GROUPS

Contributed by Troy Anthony,
Rutgers University, Class of 2018

On your own, you can only achieve so much. In a group, the possibilities are endless. While you may not have studied in groups often in high school, it is something to fully embrace in college. By studying in groups you can start the process of collaboration which is going to be critical in college and beyond. You can also solve problems and challenges much more effectively and efficiently in a group. Groups will give you an opportunity to listen and learn from the diverse members. It will prepare you well for future group projects in school and at your future internships and jobs.

LESSON 17

THERE IS NO "I" IN GROUP PROJECTS

Contributed by Carly Wilhelm,
Northeastern University, Class of 2017

If you have received a taste of group projects in high school and dread them because not every student demonstrates equal commitment, you are going to want to embrace them in college. Author's Note: From my experience as a university professor, group assignments are a critical element of every course. In some classes, the group project requires collaboration for the majority of a 14-week semester which means that you will most likely be randomly grouped with several other students for a semester long assignment. Typically, a random grouping of students includes one student who rarely participates or attends planning meetings and drops the ball when it comes to their responsibilities. On the other end of the spectrum is a student who wants to be the leader of the group, take control and dictate the plan of action. Knowing this, make every effort to mobilize your group early. While not dictating or being a bully, use your influence and persuasiveness to create a collaborative team environment where the team can flourish. Group projects are not disappearing after college. If you can master the complexities of a group assignment now, you will set yourself up for career success for many years to come.

LESSON 18

TAKE NOTE

Contributed by Troy Anthony,
Rutgers University, Class of 2018

It may seem obvious, but listen carefully and take very good notes in all your classes. Anything your professor says in class could be on a future quiz, test or final exam. Equally important, when receiving instructions for papers, projects and presentations, take detailed notes regarding every element and criteria for the final deliverable. If your professor doesn't provide enough detailed information regarding the project, speak up and ask clarifying questions and take note of the additional information they provide. If you take notes whether the old fashion way with a pen or pencil or via your tablet, you can always go back to those notes later in the day, week or semester. Those notes are going to be your roadmap to success as you navigate your way through each course through the final exam.

LESSON 19

EARN EXTRA CREDIT

Contributed by Troy Anthony,
Rutgers University, Class of 2018

There is a reason why many professors offer extra credit assignments. They want you to earn it. Take full advantage of extra credit assignments when they are offered. By earning five or more extra credit points, it could mean the difference between passing and failing or better yet, the difference between an "A" and a "B." From the first day of class, an extra credit assignment should be detailed in the class syllabus. If not, raise your hand and ask your professor if there are opportunities to earn extra credit throughout the semester. You want to ensure that you get ahead of any extra credit opportunities. Do not wait until the final class or until the professor has posted the final grades as it will be too late. Instead, be proactive when it comes to extra credit and know exactly what you can do early in the semester and earn those extra credit points. If you don't, someone else will.

LESSON 20

STUDY SOMETHING YOU LOVE

Contributed by Antonia Attardo,
Rutgers University, Class of 2019

Many who graduate high school and go to college may feel the pressure from family members persuading them convincingly what they should study and the major to declare. That is fine, but if you really don't enjoy the subject matter it could lead to struggling through your classes and not enjoying your college experience which should be an exciting and enjoyable time in your life. What's your passion? What subjects do you really love to immerse yourself in? What are you excited to study? Ask yourself those types of questions before you automatically default to what others want you to study. In today's marketplace, there is a more diverse set of occupations than ever before. More than 15 years ago, there weren't jobs with titles like social media specialist or online influencer. So, study something you love and who knows, you may create an entirely new industry or occupation.

LESSON 21

COLLEGE IS NOT ALL FUN & GAMES

Contributed by Grace Boyd-Dias,
Rutgers University, Class of 2018

Not to put a damper on your college experience, but it is not all parties, football tailgates and fun. College does require challenging yourself with course work that can be difficult while balancing a part-time job to pay the bills and an internship to set you up for success after graduation. However, you can and should have fun along the way. You can have fun in the classroom simply by being an active participant. You can have fun in a club or organization by taking a leadership role in a future event or a fundraising campaign. In other words, your college career will feature exams, projects and an endless number of stressful deadlines, but enjoy your experience to the fullest and have some fun. These four or five years may be the most fun you will have before you start your career so strike a balance between challenging yourself and having fun, and enjoy this special time in your life.

LESSON 22

CHALLENGE YOURSELF

Contributed by Alec Prieto,
Rutgers University, Class of 2018

The easiest thing to do in college is to take the simplest path, skip class when you don't feel like attending or go along with the actions of a group. Instead, when everyone else goes right, turn left. In other words, challenge yourself in everything you do - meet and make new friends, join a new club, attend an on-campus event that may take you of your comfort zone.

Author's Note: I recognize a major distinction between attending class and participating in class. Attending class is simple and easy. Proactively participating in class and engaging in conversation with your professor, guest lecturers and fellow students is challenging. Some students may be embarrassed or too shy to speak up in class. You are no longer in high school. College is the time to stand up and speak out. Those students who recognize the difference between attending a class and participating in a class and challenge themselves to participate will have an incredibly enriching college experience.

LESSON 23

NEVER LET A GRADE GET YOU DOWN

Contributed by Alec Prieto,
Rutgers University, Class of 2018

No matter how positive your mindset and how confident your out-look, you will probably fail a few tests or receive poor grades on an individual paper or group project. Throughout your college ca-reer, you will receive hundreds of assignments. You are not going to earn an "A" for each and every one, especially in your freshman and sophomore years when you are taking general electives that may have no connection to your major or stimulate your interests or intellect. Instead of mulling over a poor grade, learn from the experience and move on. Even before you move on, proactively reach out to your professor and ask if there is anything you can do to improve your grade.

Author's Note: I can't recall one instance where I did not react posi-tively to a student who took the initiative to communicate with me in a mature and responsible manner inquiring how they could do additional work to improve a grade while demonstrating their com-mitment to the course. More important than earning a few extra points is that your professor will take immediate notice and most likely collaborate more closely with you throughout the semester.

LESSON 24

SIT IN ON AS MANY CLASSES AS POSSIBLE

Contributed by Kelsey Cuje,
Rutgers University, Class of 2017

You will quickly learn that there are the classes you are required to take as electives or requirements for your major and then there are classes that you can sit in on for the pure joy of learning, networking and expanding your boundaries.

Author's Note: It wasn't until my third year of teaching when I had a student proactively email me to tell me they had heard great things about a specific class I taught or the guest speakers I brought in, and asked for permission to sit in on a class. Since that first request, I have had many more and I welcome each and every one. Not only do I respond in a positive manner but I use the opportunity to learn more about the student and their objectives and I identify a specific date for them to join our class when it will be most beneficial based on their grand plan for their transition from college to a career. I have even gone on to serve as a reference or write a letter of recommendation for several of those students who only sat in one of my classes because their desire to learn and evolve is immeasurable. Throughout your college career, look beyond your major and identify a few courses that appeal to you and simply email the professor requesting permission to join their class for a day. It will open up a new world of possibilities and opportunities.

PART III

IT'S ALL ABOUT YOU

LESSON 25

DON'T OVERCOMMIT

Contributed by Zahra Abbasi,
Rutgers University, Class of 2016

While this book highly recommends being proactive and seeking new experiences and adventures, there is a real balancing act to being a college student. There is a difference between joining a club or two and committing to far too much. From your first day on campus, you will be invited to an endless number of clubs, organizations and opportunities. You could accept all those invitations, but you will soon find yourself falling behind in your courses and that is never a good scenario. In your first year, commit to a few things that really motivate you and do them really well. Once you have a semester or two under your belt, you will have a much better sense of how many activities you can commit to beyond your classes. Like so many other things in college, only you can truly make the decision how much you can effectively manage inside and outside the classroom.

LESSON 26

THERE IS MUCH MORE TO GREEK LIFE

Contributed by Meryl Parseghian,
Rutgers University, Class of 2017

Don't believe everything you may have seen in the movies about fraternities and sororities is completely accurate. Greek life is much more than parties every night. First, you will make lifelong friends and professional contacts who you will collaborate with for the next several decades. Greek life helps you discover a sense of community within the greater campus community. Via fraternities and sororities, you will have a built-in system for everything from study buddies and school spirit to supporting charitable and philanthropic initiatives. Once you get settled after your first or second semester on campus, conduct your own research and identify a fraternity or sorority that is the right cultural fit for you.

LESSON 27

MAKE AN APPOINTMENT

Contributed by Meryl Parseghian,
Rutgers University, Class of 2017

In college, be proactive about making appointments with all of your professors, career counselors, advisors, tutors and anyone else who can assist you in optimizing your college experience. These valuable on-campus resources are there to serve and assist you. They welcome and want you to schedule an appointment for quality time outside the classroom. These appointments will provide tremendous value to you as you deal with a challenging course or navigate the nuances of securing an internship. However, only you can make that appointment. No one else can take that critical step for you so be proactive, make appointments and get the most out of all the resources your college offers.

LESSON 28

SEEK HELP

Contributed by Meryl Parseghian,
Rutgers University, Class of 2017

Every student needs help and assistance from time-to-time. It's only natural. From tutors and academic advisors to career counselors and professors, there are many great resources on every college campus where you can seek advice and counsel. Never hesitate to proactively seek help for any personal or academic challenge you are attempting to solve. Solutions come faster when you collaborate with trusted resources. While college can be a fun and exciting, it also presents a wide variety of challenges for each and every student and without mom and dad at your side, turn to experts and professionals on campus who are eager to identify solutions for your unique situation.

LESSON 29

FIND THE FREE STUFF

Contributed by Meryl Parseghian,
Rutgers University, Class of 2017

From your first day on campus for freshman orientation, the unofficial welcome committee may be distributing a variety of samples from school apparel and merchandise to notebooks and pens. It's just the beginning. As you manage your budget efficiently, take advantage of freebies and samples. You are a highly coveted demographic. Companies and brands have an interest in engaging you and sampling their products so there is no reason not to give them a test drive. Typically at high traffic areas including the student center and major sports events you will find companies distributing samples. Also, use that student identification card to your advantage. It may offer discounts on campus as well at stores and restaurants in the larger community. You are a college student living on a limited budget so there is nothing wrong with freebies, discounts and special offers that were intended for you.

LESSON 30

BE AN ACTIVE PARTICIPANT

Contributed by Jesse Ruela,
Penn State University, Class of 2016

Before you ever step on campus, you can begin a level of participation that will make your college experience highly rewarding. In other words, be an active participant every day, every semester, every year in classrooms, clubs, extracurricular activities and even the community where your university is located. Too many graduates look back on their college years and express regret that they did not participate more. Don't make the same mistake or have the same regrets. You can easily get caught up in the demands of your course work and ignore everything your school has to offer you. Instead, try to strike a balance between your classes and your participation as a proud student of the institution of higher learning that you attend.

LESSON 31

BE A LEADER

Contributed by Emma Sinanan,
Pace University, Class of 2018

One of the easiest things to do in college is to follow the pack. When your roommates decide they don't want to answer the alarm and attend an 8:30 a.m. class, it's so easy to crawl back under the covers and follow their lead. Don't do it. Before you step on campus, make a commitment that you are going to be a leader and not a follower. It's not an easy commitment to make. If it was, everyone would do it.

Author's Note: If you consistently lead by your actions and words, you will inspire a following. I can promise you that because I have witnessed leaders in and outside the classroom and they earn the respect of their fellow students, professors and advisors.

LESSON 32

GET ORGANIZED

Contributed by Carly Galasso,
Rutgers University, Class of 2018

While you are in high school, you have a wide variety of assistants to help keep you organized starting with mom and dad followed by the teachers who you meet with each and every day. Unless you plan to attend one of the service academies, you don't have a designated organizer in college to keep you on a tight schedule. That responsibility falls on you. If you have a class that only meets once a week, you will only see your professor once a week not like your high school teachers who you met five times a week. Make it a top priority to be as organized as possible in the way you manage your courses and other activities. Whether it's a master calendar in your dorm room, file organizers, different colored notebooks for each class or daily "to-do" lists, do whatever it is you need to do to be as organized as possible before you even step on campus.

LESSON 33

INVEST IN YOURSELF

Contributed by Alyssa Dell'Acqua,
Charleston Southern University, Class of 2019

Throughout college you will have friends, classmates and roommates come and go. Some will remain with you throughout your time on campus while others may transfer or even drop out of school. While you will invest your time and efforts into developing friendships, never forget that the greatest investment you must make is in yourself. In other words, be selfish when it comes to investing in your evolution throughout your college years. With respect to your growth and advancement, invest in you as much as you are able. It may mean skipping the party everyone is going to because there is an opportunity to network with a guest speaker that night on campus or it might mean never missing that 8:30 a.m. class while your roommates sleep until noon.

Author's Note: For me, it was the opportunity to gain experience working in the press box at our home football games while my roommates enjoyed tailgating. I was tempted to call in sick but the investment I made in collaborating with sports journalists and broadcasters played a critical role in securing my first job after graduation and a 30-year career in public relations.

LESSON 34

MAKE AN IMPACT

Contributed by Austin Sommerer,
Penn State University, Class of 2017

While you could easily sleep your way through your college years by just getting by in your classes and participating minimally in extracurricular activities, you would be wasting your time. Instead, go out of your way to make an impact each and every semester. You should never think that your voice is too small to be heard or your actions are too minor to have an impact. There are so many ways to make an impact in college - start a new club, lead a fundraising effort, befriend someone who appears to feel out of place, mobilize your friends and roommates for a good cause. There truly are many opportunities and organizations on every campus in the nation that are eager to have students join, support and deliver impact in a way that betters the campus and the entire college community.

LESSON 35

FORGE YOUR OWN PATH

Contributed by Austin Sommerer,
Penn State University, Class of 2017

No two students are the same and no two paths to graduation are identical. No matter how many thousands of students are on your campus, you are an individual with your own thoughts, goals, concerns and passions. Use all of those things and many more to forge your own unique college journey. From your classes to your clubs to the friends you make, forge your own unique path to graduation. Do something for the first time. Start a new organization, club or charitable cause at your college that no one ever thought of. In other words, be a pioneer, explorer, and a leader of your fellow students.

LESSON 36

SET YOURSELF UP FOR SUCCESS

Contributed by Jenifer Elizondo,
Rutgers University, Class of 2018

In college, you have every chance to succeed and plenty of opportunities to fail. It's all up to you. No one person will have a greater influence on the success you achieve in college than you. Only you can make the decision if you are going to attend class or skip. Of course, if you skip, you are not setting yourself up for success. Only you can make the decision whether you are going to procrastinate and wait until the last minute to research and write a final paper or set yourself up for success by proactively starting the paper the day the professor assigns it. In everything you do in college from your course work to securing internship experience, set yourself up for success. Be proactive, ask questions and get ahead of the calendar. For example, if you have your sights on a summer internship, set yourself up for success by speaking to your contacts in January during winter break and scheduling informational meetings and interviews as opposed to taking action in May when most summer internships are already filled. You can't spell success without "u" and it's "you" who will create your own success.

LESSON 37

SLEEP WELL

Contributed by Troy Anthony,
Rutgers University, Class of 2018

There is a difference between sleeping in and sleeping well. If you go to sleep in the early hours of the morning and wake up at noon, you probably did not sleep well. Quality sleep is critical to your health and wellness throughout college. Just like you plan your time for classes, studying and extracurricular activities, plan your sleep. Quality sleep will help you remain alert and focused in class and it will reduce the number of days you just don't feel that great. Quality sleep will help make your college years a much more rewarding and enjoyable experience than four years of late nights, early mornings and cat naps.

LESSON 38

EXERCISE YOUR BODY AS WELL AS YOUR MIND

Contributed by Jacqueline Manza,
Northwestern State University, Class of 2019

Most college campuses are filled with scenic running and cycling trails and fitness facilities so don't let them go to waste. While you may be focused on exercising your mind in the classroom, one of the best ways to keep those creative and strategic brain cells fully engaged is to run, swim, lift, or join a fitness class or even better yet, some sort of club or intramural sport. All of our minds need exercise. It's why we had recess as kids to force us to get out of the classroom. You now are on a campus where you have fitness, exercise and sports opportunities right outside your door. In those first few weeks on campus, familiarize yourself with the fitness facilities and encourage your roommates to join you and start a fitness routine. I promise you that a fitness break will help your mind write that paper you have been challenged to finish or complete that group project you've been putting on hold. Fitness will fuel your mind.

LESSON 39

SET GOALS EVERY SEMESTER

Contributed by Samantha Franco,
Rutgers University, Class of 2018

While your ultimate goal is to graduate and secure that dream job, consider every semester a goal-setting opportunity. As you begin your freshman year, it is challenging to look four years down the road at only one or two major objectives. To build up to that graduation day, set goals for each and every semester. If you want to take it one step further, set daily, weekly and monthly goals each semester. There are some obvious goals for each semester - make the Dean's List, earn an "A" in every class, but go beyond the classroom in your goal setting. Set your sights on achieving measurable goals such as expanding your professional network by a specific number of contacts, securing that internship you have been talking about for a semester or two, or finally running for a leadership position in a club in which you are already a member. It is these semester milestones that will ladder up to graduation day.

LESSON 40

ARTICULATE YOUR ARGUMENT

Contributed by Rebecca Shapiro,
Rutgers University, Class of 2018

While you may never join your university's debate team, you are going to need to learn how to articulate your argument and point-of-view in college and beyond. Aside from formally standing in front of the class in a public speaking course or delivering a final presentation, you will be faced with many opportunities to articulate your position on a specific topic with confidence. It may be trying to convince your professor that you earned an "A" as opposed to a "B+" or it might be the time when you need to persuade your club's members to elect you president, or it will be when you have to articulate to a company or organization why you are the strongest candidate for that full-time job after graduation. If you enter college afraid or shy to speak your mind with confidence and conviction, you will need to get over that feeling and fast. Make every effort as soon as you start college to improve and evolve your public speaking whether in a one-on-one session or before a group. It will pay tremendous dividends for the remainder of your college years and throughout your career.

LESSON 41

PURSUE YOUR PASSIONS

Contributed by Reid Burch,
Loyola University Maryland, Class of 2018

Aside from studying subjects you love, pursue your passions outside the classroom. Most colleges offer an endless amount of opportunities to pursue your passions and thrive with others who have the same passions. Whether it's fashion, photography, sports, music, theater, film, video games, graphic design or food, pursue it. Take the first step in your first semester and research and identify the clubs, teams or organizations that cater to individuals like you who have a passion for a specific subject. Then, take that next step and attend your first meeting to learn more. Finally, be an active participant, not just an attending member. You will ultimately find yourself collaborating with individuals who have the same passion, forming bonds and friendships that will last a lifetime.

Author's Note: I am a perfect example. I had a passion for broadcasting, joined the student radio station and 30 years later, have friendships that never would have started if I did not take those first few simple steps and attend a meeting. That's all it took.

LESSON 42

BE PROUD OF YOU

Contributed by Reid Burch,
Loyola University Maryland, Class of 2018

While many people from family and friends to classmates and professors will be eager to help you throughout your college career, never forget that ultimately, most decisions   will come down to one person - you. Be proud and confident of yourself from that first day on campus. Look in the mirror every day and tell yourself you are going to win the day. Never lack confidence or doubt yourself as you meet new people or take on challenging assignments. If you make a mistake or fail, learn from the experience and move on. Your college can offer you as many courses, clubs and activities as one person can handle, but you first have to be proud of the person you are so that you can take full advantage of everything college is offering.

LESSON 43

CONTROL WHAT YOU CAN CONTROL

Contributed by Caroline Petrone,
University of South Carolina, Class of 2017

In college, there are a variety of things that may be out of your control like how fast that required course filled up before you were able to register. However, don't let those uncontrollable things upset you or cause you to shift your mind away from what is really important in achieving those semester-by-semester objectives. Instead, control what you can control. For example, you control whether you attend class or take the easy way out and skip. No one else controls that decision other than you. There is also no one who can prevent you from being proactive in joining a club or attending an event on campus. There is no one who forces you to procrastinate in completing an assignment or prevents you from studying for an exam. All those things are well within your control so take complete control of your college career and great things will result.

LESSON 44

GET INVOLVED IN THE COMMUNITY

Contributed by Caroline Petrone,
University of South Carolina, Class of 2017

Your college experience should go well beyond your classes and your campus. Your college or university is most likely a critical part of a larger community so look beyond campus to the community where your school is located and look for ways to get involved. At many colleges, the athletic department and teams have community-based programs where student-athletes volunteer their time in the community throughout the academic year. You don't need to be an athlete to invest some of your time in the community. There are most likely charitable events you can support or even help manage and produce. There are small businesses and non-profits that would love to have college students serve as interns where you can gain real-world experience that goes on your resume. Once you have settled onto campus and figured your way around, branch out a bit further and discover the local community. There is a world of opportunity just a few steps from your dorm room where your involvement in the community will amplify your college experience.

LESSON 45

LISTEN TO YOURSELF

Contributed by Daijie Yuan,
Rutgers University, Class of 2017

In high school, you may have caved to peer pressure and listened to the advice of friends or been persuaded by the point-of-view of a negative influence. In college, make a commitment to listen to yourself, your instincts, your conscious. You can gather as much information and insights as you need from classmates, professors and advisors, but ultimately, you need to make the decision that is best for you based on what you are telling yourself. No one else can make a decision for you. Only you know what is best based on your unique journey and objectives so listen closely to what your heart and mind are telling you and take action.

LESSON 46

TAKE A CHANCE

Contributed by Pat Kelly,
Rutgers University, Class of 2017

Do you consider yourself a risk taker? Do you like to take a chance on something and see where it may take you? If so, college is the place for you. Your college years should be filled with an endless number of opportunities to take chances. You can be a calculated risk taker. In other words, take a chance, try something new and evaluate the result. You don't need to take chances with a high degree of risk or reward, but you can take chances on things that might improve your approach to course work or open the door to a job or internship. Take chances throughout college, evaluate your experience and apply what you have learned to the next time you consider taking a chance on an opportunity.

LESSON 47

FIND YOUR MOTIVATION

Contributed by Pat Kelly,
Rutgers University, Class of 2017

What motivates you? What gets you excited? What drives you? What inspires you? If you can answer those questions you will be able to find your motivation. It may be a passion - sports, fashion, music - or it may be something cause related or a role in leadership. As you start college, it is critical to truly understand what motivates you and not your parents or friends. You are the one who is going to attend and participate in your college experience for the next four or five years. It's not your parents or other family members. With that, you want to immerse yourself in courses, clubs and extracurricular activities that motivate you to be the best you that you can be.

LESSON 48

HAVE A CONVERSATION WITH YOUR SENIOR SELF

Contributed by Rachel Boyce,
Stockton University, Class of 2018

Where do you want to be in four years? What type of job do you want to secure? What are you going to need to do to reach your objectives? Don't wait until the final semester of senior year to ask and answer these questions. Rather, start as soon as you arrive on campus for freshman year and continuously ask yourself these questions and many more as you progress through school. In other words, have a conversation with your future self. Use each semester and each milestone to revisit the conversation. Some of the questions may be similar but the answers will vary based on your personal development. More important, this conversation with your future self will help you identify the path you need to take to reach your objectives and the actions you need to take along the way to get there. You may not have all the answers to your own questions, but if you ask the same questions to professors and mentors, you will receive the guidance and counsel to set you up for success by the time you receive your diploma.

LESSON 49

CONTINUOUSLY WRITE THE WRONG

Contributed by Lexi Amato,
Emerson College, Class of 2019

You can never perfect the art of writing. Write, write and write some more. If you consider writing a weakness, don't run away from it. You may not be a journalism major, but writing will play a major role in your college experience and the ability to write effectively and error-free will only increase following graduation. Starting with your freshman year, take advantage of any writing labs on campus, writing tutors and professors who are more than willing to take quality time to review a writing assignment before, during and after the paper has been submitted and graded. Make every effort to learn from each writing assignment and apply those learnings to the next one. During the summer between freshman and sophomore years, look into taking a writing course at a local community college even if it is not for credit or join any type of club where writing is at heart of the club's mission. You may start to love writing so much that you join the student newspaper or a creative writing society. The more you write, the better your writing will become and the more success you will have in college and beyond.

LESSON 50

SPEAK OUT PUBLICLY

Contributed by Kelsey Cuje,
Rutgers University, Class of 2017

While many of us enter college with anxiety about public speaking, use the next four years to transform yourself into a confident public speaker. No matter your major, I believe that public speaking should be a mandatory course for every college student. Whether speaking confidently to one individual in an internship or job interview or making a presentation to dozens of your classmates or eventually your colleagues at work, public speaking, like writing, will be something you will do for the rest of your life and the more comfortable and confident you feel in doing it, the more success you will experience. While in college, seek opportunities to speak regularly in front of audiences. Investigate joining the debate club or stop by the student radio station and learn if there is an opportunity to be a news reader, sportscaster or disc jockey. The more opportunities you create for yourself to speak out, the more natural it will feel to stand before an audience and articulate your thoughts in a meaningful and confident manner.

LESSON 51

JOIN OR START A CLUB

Contributed by Kelsey Cuje,
Rutgers University, Class of 2017

It may sound like a bit of old school advice, but the quickest way to immerse yourself in the college experience beyond your classes and your dorm room is to join several clubs and then eventually start your own club. Most schools make it very easy to join a club as the clubs typically make themselves well known during student orientation. Even if this is not the case at your college, seek out the clubs that match your passions and interests. Whether that passion is playing video games as eSports teams have become very popular in the past few years or a cause related organization or the student-run public relations agency, every club on campus seeks new members. It is today's freshman who will be tomorrow's club leaders. Clubs offer a chance for you to interact and engage with other students on a consistent basis on a subject matter in which all members have a common interest. Once you have experienced a few clubs for a year or two and better understand how meetings are run, budgets are managed and objectives are achieved, start your own club your junior year. It's a great opportunity to demonstrate leadership and an entrepreneurial spirit, and will also look great on your resume and be a compelling talking point when you go for that internship or job interview.

LESSON 52

PUT DOWN YOUR PHONE

Contributed by Paige Daly,
University of New Haven, Class of 2020

There's a whole new world out there when you arrive on campus. If you keep your head down, staring at your mobile phone, you are going to miss the next four years and some amazing experiences that are going to pass right on by you. Make a real effort to put down your phone, shut it off and look up at your fellow students, professors and opportunities that will make your college career the most it can be. I promise you that there will be plenty of time to text, tweet and post. It just doesn't need to be all the time. When you arrive in class, turn off your phone and fully immerse yourself in your course for the hour or more that you are there. Instead of just attending a club meeting and glimpsing at your phone every few minutes, shut down your phone and be an active participant. If you can control the use of your phone and not let your phone control you, you will have a much more fulfilling college experience.

LESSON 53

IMMERSE YOURSELF IN-PERSON

Contributed by Alec Prieto,
Rutgers University, Class of 2018

In today's digital society, it can be very easy to become too reliant on technology throughout your college career. From taking online classes to emailing your professor to utilizing virtual help desks, technology has made it too easy to make the college experience less personal. Author's Note: A recent guest speaker in my class said we need a bit less Artificial Intelligence (AI) and a lot more Human Interaction (HI). With that, buck the trend and put your own personal touch on your unique college experience. Instead of emailing a professor for assistance, request office hours and the opportunity to have a one-on-one conversation. Rather than viewing a livestream of a guest speaker or special event on campus, rally some friends and immerse yourself in the experience. Technology is great, but there is nothing more rewarding and productive than in-person interaction, engagement and experiences.

LESSON 54

MANAGING YOUR TIME IS THE FOUNDATION FOR SUCCESS

Contributed by Alec Prieto,
Rutgers University, Class of 2018

If you have never heard of the term, "time management," know it, learn it and excel at it. Effective time management will not only set you up for success in college but it will be a critical component of a successful career. Attending classes, studying for tests, writing papers, participating in clubs, working part-time and interning all at the same time is not impossible. Hundreds of thousands of students have done it very effectively in the past and many more will do it in the future. The key is managing your time in a highly effective manner. If you tend to procrastinate or are challenged multi-tasking, get ahead of the curve even before your first day on campus. Inquire with your school if they offer information or a time management advisor or mini-course. If you know someone - a parent, older sibling or high school classmate - who excels in time management ask them for their tips and tricks and any advice they would offer a new college student. A few weeks into a semester, managing assignments and tests in five courses can be challenging for even the most effective manager of time and can lead to failure for those who mismanage their time. Be proactive when it comes to time management, seek a variety of recommendations and then customize the time management plan that will work best for your unique schedule.

LESSON 55

PUT HIGH SCHOOL IN THE PAST

Contributed by Zahra Abbasi,
Rutgers University, Class of 2016

Don't live in the past. Don't consistently reminisce about the glory days of high school. You are starting to write a new chapter in your life and this chapter can stand alone. Of course you can stay in contact with high school friends, but fully embrace college. For many students, it's the first time living away from home which means it's a time for a new start in a new city or town with new classmates and future friends. For those who may be staying home and attending community college, take the same mindset. Just because you didn't move out of your mom and dad's house doesn't mean attending community college isn't a new and exciting experience. No matter where you attend college, live and flourish in the present.

LESSON 56

REBRAND YOURSELF

Contributed by Kasey Chan,
Rutgers University, Class of 2018

No matter what you were known for in high school or how you were labeled - nerd, jock, cheerleader, band geek, teacher's pet or troublemaker - it does not matter. When you get to college, rebrand yourself. Don't be what others label you as. Instead, be who you want to be and rebrand yourself. College is a time to establish and evolve your personal brand. You get to make the decision what your brand represents. Once you establish your brand philosophy and values, live it and embody it inside and outside the classroom. As your personal brand evolves, you will attract followers and like-minded supporters.

LESSON 57

CONNECT WITH UPPERCLASSMEN

Contributed by Avery McWilliams,
Rutgers University, Class of 2017

When you first arrive on campus, you will be intimidated just to connect with your own classmates, but it is critical that as you immerse yourself in your freshman year that you create real connections with upperclassmen. Why? Upperclassmen were in your shoes just a few years ago and have experienced everything that is ahead of you. Via clubs or other organizations, meet upperclassmen and seek their advice, learn from their mistakes, and soak up as much information and knowledge as you can about their college experience. They won't even realize that they can serve as a wise sage whose wisdom could set you up for success. Just imagine, by connecting with upperclassmen, you gain access to their college playbook including the plays that worked and those that backfired. That is one powerful book to get your hands on freshman year.

LESSON 58

YOU DON'T NEED TO BE THE NEXT ZUCKERBERG

Contributed by Alec Prieto,
Rutgers University, Class of 2018

No matter how much pressure you may get from family, your college experience does not need to result in the launch of the next great start-up or a high paying job following graduation. Your journey through college should result in the greatest version of you. Pursue your passions and immerse yourself in your interests and great things will result.

Author's Note: Having taught nearly a thousand university students and mentored many more, I can promise you that no two journeys through college are alike. In fact, you really should set your sights on setting your own curriculum and path. If your university allows, take the time to develop your own independent study or even your own course. When you enter the second semester of freshman year, be one of the few who secures an internship in your area of study while most of your roommates will fall back on a summer job of life guarding or waiting tables. College does not need to result in you being the next Mark Zuckerberg. It should transform you into the greatest version of you.

LESSON 59

GET SERIOUS ABOUT SOCIAL MEDIA

Contributed by Kimberly Jones,
Rutgers University, Class of 2017

In high school or perhaps even in middle school, you were introduced to a new language called "social media" and you were fluent by the time you graduated. Well, the language of social media will become an even bigger part of your life in college. However, you now need to get serious about social media. In other words, start using your Twitter, Facebook, Instagram and Snapchat channels to your advantage. As you gain a better sense of what industry you plan to enter after college start to shift your social media content from fun and friends to the future. As you enter your sophomore year of college, produce and distribute content about your future career and occupation. If you can start to generate consistent content about the industry you are interested in, future employers will take notice when you interview for jobs in a few years.

LESSON 60

CLEAN UP YOUR SOCIAL MEDIA

Contributed by Ashley DeSalvatore,
Rutgers University, Class of 2016

A lot of the content you produce and share on social media in your first or second year of college may be fun and harmless, but that same content in junior or senior year may result in a future employer selecting another candidate based on what they saw on Twitter. As you start college, seriously consider your content marketing strategy via your owned media channels. As students get serious about the future industry in which they plan to work, they create professional social media channels that highlight news, trends and their own insights regarding that specific industry. In other words, they may keep their personal channels private and make their professional channels public facing. If you can get a head start your freshman or sophomore year on launching a Twitter channel that focuses exclusively on a specific industry or passion point, future employers will not only take notice but they will be impressed.

PART IV

LOOKING AHEAD TO YOUR CAREER

LESSON 61

THINK LONG-TERM

Contributed by Ari Gutman,
Rutgers University, Class of 2017

You have just started your college career and it's hard to think past your first classes, first club meetings and first social events and immersing yourself in a new life experience. After you get through that initial wave of firsts, take a deep breath and give thought to long-term goals and ambitions. Ultimately, you are attending college to secure a job after graduation and prepare for a career. With that as a long-term goal, think that way as you go about your daily classes and interactions with professors and other influencers. In other words, use some of your vision to look beyond the next class, test and group project and to future internships, experiences and opportunities.

LESSON 62

NETWORKING STARTS FRESHMAN YEAR

Contributed by Stephen Moodie,
Rutgers University, Class of 2016

From your very first day on campus, you should be networking. Believe it or not, your freshman year roommates and classmates will be senior level executives and decision makers in another decade or two. Officially begin your professional networking career the first day you step on campus and start with your fellow students and then extend your networking to your professors, guest lecturers and eventually, professionals who you meet in your career area of interest. When you go home for a weekend or for the holidays, take a proactive approach to meeting people who could influence decisions you make about your future career including internship opportunities. Neighbors and extended family members who you may have not paid too much attention to in the past could in fact be the point of contact that sets you on the right course for your career after college.

LESSON 63

BEGIN RESEARCHING YOUR FUTURE CAREER IMMEDIATELY

Contributed by Melissa Jannuzzi,
Rutgers University, Class of 2017

It's never too early to starting researching what industry you may want to enter after graduation. As a freshman, you are probably thinking that you just want to research where the book store is located so that you can purchase all the required reading you need for your first semester, but you will be a senior before you know it. Try not to use the excuse that you still need to declare your major or that you are undecided as that excuse has a short shelf-life. Starting freshman year, visit a career advisor on campus and learn what services they offer students, even first-year students. If you have adjunct professors who also work full-time ask them about their profession and also take advantage of guest lecturers as they can serve as a great source of information regarding a future career in a variety of industries. If you can gather information early, it will make that first internship before your sophomore year more relevant and meaningful. It will also enable you to eliminate occupations you don't want to pursue.

LESSON 64

GET WORK EXPERIENCE SOONER THAN LATER

Contributed by Melissa Jannuzzi,
Rutgers University, Class of 2017

For many college students, the lightbulb doesn't go on until the second semester of their junior year when they realize that they should probably start securing some sort of relevant real world experience knowing that one year later they will be graduating and seeking that first job. Don't wait until junior or senior year to start gaining internship experience. In fact, I highly recommend that you gain experience relevant to your course work before you even take your first college course. And, don't use the excuse that you need a part-time job to pay your bills. You can attend college, have a part-time job and gain internship experience.

Author's Note: I paid my way through college by parking cars all four years, but I earned my first job after high school graduation by interning as a writer at a daily newspaper before I started taking college courses and I continued interning every semester with relevant organizations in the media and communications industry. Finally, it's not mandatory for an internship to be full-time or five days a week. Some of my best internship experiences were for a couple of hours a day a few days a week right on campus. Internships and relevant experiences are right in front of you. You just need to open your eyes, demonstrate a proactive mindset and grab the opportunity.

LESSON 65

BEING UNDECIDED IS NOT UNUSUAL

Contributed by Kasey Chan,
Rutgers University, Class of 2018

Very few students arrive on campus and know exactly what they want to study and where they want to work after graduation. It is fine if you are undecided about your major or what industry you want to enter in four or five years. However, don't let that indecision be an excuse as you trek through freshman and sophomore years. If you are undecided about your declared major, don't sit back waiting for some sort of inspiration to arrive one day. Instead, use your first year on campus to conduct field research and ask as many people as many questions as you are able. Take quality time to speak to seniors who were in your shoes just a few years earlier, sit in on classes that may interest you and meet with career advisors on campus. The more information you proactively gather will empower you to go from indecision to making a confident decision about your future.

LESSON 66

RECRUIT YOUR RESOURCES

Contributed by Meryl Parseghian,
Rutgers University, Class of 2017

It may be challenging to think about this as you just start your college career, but you are going to want to start proactively recruiting your resources and not wait until senior year. In other words, you want to start aligning a wide variety of resources and individuals who can serve as your support system throughout your college career and beyond. From formal mentors to informal advisors and counselors, the network you establish and evolve will help you navigate college, internships and ultimately, your career. Resources can range from family, friends and neighbors to professors and upperclassmen who have already been through everything you are going to experience. Your network will serve as an invaluable resource. However, you will only get as much out of it as you proactively contribute, so maintain regular contact with these critical resources and once in a while, proactively ask your resources if you can assist them in any way.

LESSON 67

MASTER LINKEDIN

Contributed by Alec Prieto,
Rutgers University, Class of 2018

Of course you are probably fluent in Snapchat and Instagram, but LinkedIn is the digital networking platform that you most likely are not aware of prior to your freshman year and the one you need to master by the time you graduate. Think of LinkedIn as the Facebook or Instagram for professional networking. Like your social media channels that required time to amass followers, the same is true for LinkedIn. You do not want to launch your LinkedIn channel the week before graduation. Instead, launch it as you start college. There are an endless amount of online recommendations instructing how to create and optimize your LinkedIn profile. Once you do that, simply start by sending a LinkedIn invitation to family members and neighbors who are immersed in their careers and then extend the invitation to upperclassmen who you know who may have already established a profile. If you can become fluent in LinkedIn at the start of your freshman year, you will want to send an invitation to everyone you meet throughout your college career - professors, guest lecturers, academic advisors, internship supervisors - so that by the time you are a senior, you have a robust network of allies who will be eager to assist you as you seek that first job after graduation.

LESSON 68

STAY CURRENT

Contributed by Kelsey Cuje,
Rutgers University, Class of 2017

There is a whole other world outside your campus. Try to avoid becoming so isolated that you lose contact with the outside world and all that is happening. Current events and pop culture will impact your current studies and future trajectory in one way or another. Take a few minutes each day to scan the news beyond just the student newspaper. Follow a wide variety of news, entertainment and sports handles via your Twitter platform and check each morning before you head out to class so that you can be armed with knowledge and information to participate in conversations that go beyond your text books. As you advance to your sophomore year and beyond and become more focused on the industry you one day hope to work in, follow the trade media for that industry. Simply subscribe to the online trade media platforms and follow their Twitter channels and you will be well versed when the time comes for internship interviews and professional networking.

LESSON 69

READY YOUR RESUME FRESHMAN YEAR

Contributed by Kate Galgano,
The College of New Jersey, Class of 2019

Too many students put off the development of their resume until they are formally applying for full-time work in their final year of college. Your resume should be a work in progress starting your freshman year. By seeking advice on resume writing early in your college career and reviewing the resumes of seniors or recent graduates, you will have a much better understanding of the type of experience you need to secure over the next four years to set you apart in a competitive job market. If you know of one or more family members or friends who recently graduated college and earned their first job, ask to review their resume and use their template as your guide. By taking this approach, it will force you to secure internship experience early on in your college career and motivate you to continuously update and strengthen your resume. It also provides you the opportunity to share your resume regularly with professionals in your network throughout your college career who will offer solid advice on how to improve and evolve in a way that differentiates you from other future graduates.

PART V

PHILOSOPHY 101

LESSON 70

BE NICE

Contributed by Kimberly Jones,
Rutgers University, Class of 2017

There is no lesson more simply stated in this book, but it's a powerful one. From the first day you arrive on campus, be nice to your roommates, classmates, professors and anyone you interact with. Yes, you will find yourself stressed, confused, disappointed and even angry at times, but if you are genuinely nice to others, it will attract and engage many more people than if you go through your college years mad at the world. You can be the smartest person on campus but if you are not nice, people will distance themselves from you just the same way co-workers distance themselves from individuals with negative attitudes at the workplace. Wake up every day of your college career and commit to being nice to others and great things will result.

LESSON 71

TRANSFERRING CAN BE TERRIFIC

Contributed by Grace Boyd-Dias,
Rutgers University, Class of 2018

Many students go to college and realize less than a semester into their freshman year that they made a mistake in the school they selected. Perhaps it is too far from home and now they understand that they want to be closer to family and friends or they now have a better sense of what they want to study and there are other universities that offer more robust programs in the major they plan to declare. No matter the reason, transferring to a different school does not represent making a mistake or failing. It is actually a sign that you are maturing and evolving and that is a very good thing. Once you arrive at your new school, don't label yourself as a "transfer student." Forget the past and look ahead to the future at your new school.

LESSON 72

IT DOESN'T REQUIRE A PARTY TO HAVE FUN

Contributed by Grace Boyd-Dias,
Rutgers University, Class of 2018

For years, there have been rankings of the top party schools. Let me let you in on a little secret - you don't have to attend a party to have fun in college. The amount of extracurricular activities that offer fun and exciting experiences on and off campus is endless and too many to list on this page, but here are a few - attend a college football game on a Saturday in late September, listen to an entertaining guest speaker at the college student center on a Monday night, participate in a charitable fundraising event with your classmates and feel great about contributing to a worthy cause, stand in the student section of your school's basketball team and cheer, enjoy a battle-of-the-bands concert or an acapella competition on-campus. Each and every day, there is an opportunity to have fun on campus. You just need to seek these opportunities out and be a bit of an explorer.

LESSON 73

THERE IS NO SUCH THING AS BEING POPULAR

Contributed by Grace Boyd-Dias,
Rutgers University, Class of 2018

In high school, there is always the most popular person or the popular group. You can leave all that behind when you get to college. Universities are just too diverse and there are just so many interesting and exciting people for you to interact and engage with that popularity was left behind the day you graduated high school. Don't focus on being part of the popular or in-crowd as it doesn't exist. Instead, focus on creating your own in-crowd whether that's in the classroom or on the weekends. There are no barriers to meeting and interacting with new people. Every day at college should serve as an opportunity to expand your social network. Instead of focusing on popularity, concentrate on diversity and a dynamic series of diverse relationships with people of all ages, genders and backgrounds.

LESSON 74

DON'T JUDGE

Contributed by Grace Boyd-Dias,
Rutgers University, Class of 2018

As you step onto campus, consider it a no-judgement zone. In other words, forget the judging you may have done in high school about the way people dressed or cut their hair. You are joining a diverse campus community where there is no room or tolerance for judging people. Instead of judging, use college as the opportunity to conduct research and learn about people. Act like a journalist and get into the routine of asking people about their background, ambitions, goals and future. If you can replace judging others with learning about others, you will open doors to new and unexpected relationships, opportunities and possibilities. College can be your training ground for taking this new approach to embracing diversity and you can then carry it through to your career where it will empower you.

LESSON 75

PROCRASTINATION IS YOUR ENEMY

Contributed by Dana Carbone,
Monmouth University Class, of 2018

No matter how many weeks you have until a paper is due or a group project needs to be submitted, don't wait. From the moment you receive an assignment that has more than a one week deadline, jump on it immediately. You may not be able to have control over a surprise quiz, but you have complete control over every assignment with a deadline.

Author's Note: I design my courses in a way that the entire course including the syllabus, future readings, discussion boards and assignments are all online from the first day of class. I encourage students to look ahead and if they feel confident and comfortable with taking on a future assignment, they don't need to wait until the week it is actually assigned. This was one of my greatest learnings when I studied for my master's degree and it eliminated any influence that the enemy I like to call "procrastination" may have had.

LESSON 76

BE PRACTICAL

Contributed by Carly Galasso,
Rutgers University, Class of 2018

Moving cross-country to attend a major university may sound incredibly exciting, but does it really make sense? Is it really practical? Something that may sound a lot less exciting and glamorous is to drive five miles to the local community college, attend class for a year or two and then transfer to a four-year university. As mentioned in this book several times, each and every college student is on their own unique journey and that journey begins before they ever step foot on campus. There are many considerations - costs, area of focus, proximity to home - and many others. What should not be a consideration is impressing your friends or relatives. Try to avoid getting caught up in attending the big university with the big price tag especially if you are still trying to understand what you are interested in studying and what you may want to do after graduation. It's alright not to know. In fact, I would guess that the majority of 17 and 18-years olds are undecided when it comes to truly knowing what they want to study, but the pressure of senior year of high school and all that goes with it can get the best of them. Instead, be confident to admit you don't have all the answers and be practical in your decision making.

LESSON 77

RELAX & BREATHE

Contributed by Carly Galasso,
Rutgers University, Class of 2018

There are many times throughout your college career when you will feel completely overwhelmed. It is natural and normal. Simply relax and breathe and take inventory of the tasks in front of you and how you will achieve them. I am a big believer in compartmentalizing everything that seems impossible to get done. It's a great part of the "relax and breathe exercise." Take 10 minutes of "me time" and map out everything that needs to be achieved whenever you are struck with the feeling of being overwhelmed. Once you have listed all your tasks, begin to prioritize based on the deadline date for each task and the time required to complete each task. Of course, it's not as simple as completing one task at a time knowing you have as many as five classes and other activities occurring simultaneously, but this mapping and prioritization approach will leave you less stressed and prepared to achieve what you once believe may have been impossible.

LESSON 78

USE STRESS TO YOUR ADVANTAGE

Contributed by Gedalya Gerstle,
Rutgers University, Class of 2018

Aside from all the fun times you will enjoy in college, there will be many moments of stress. It's just natural when you are juggling five or six classes and they all have final projects and exams occurring simultaneously. Use that stress to your advantage. For example if stress is preventing you from sleeping or has you waking up extra early, use that time to your advantage and find a quiet place on campus where you can immerse yourself in your work. Channel your stress into positive energy. Don't run away from it. Stress presents an opportunity to take inventory of your assignments and deadlines and prioritize everything you need to complete. Stress can serve as a major motivator if you just use it to your advantage.

LESSON 79

FAILING DOESN'T MAKE YOU A FAILURE

Contributed by Gedalya Gerstle,
Rutgers University, Class of 2018

You will fail in college – in the classroom and outside the classroom. In the classroom, whether it's a pop quiz that catches you off guard or that first paper where your writing style just didn't match what the professor was expecting, you will mostly likely fail at least one assignment. That may have never happened to you in high school. Just because you fail a college quiz, project, paper or even a personal relationship, doesn't make you a failure. In fact, it is how you learn and respond to that failure that will set you on a course for success in college. Instead of running away from a failed assignment, face it head-on. Immediately schedule time with your professor to review your mistakes and demonstrate a desire to learn. Use the opportunity to request an extra credit assignment. Finally, apply your learning to the next paper or test and improve on your past performance. Your future college success will emerge from past failures.

LESSON 80

SPEND WISELY

Contributed by Ashley DeSalvatore,
Rutgers University, Class of 2016

While some of the lessons in this book are philosophical in nature, this one is as practical as it gets. You are now a college student. You are not expected to have disposable income to do what you wish. In fact, you may be working a part-time or full-time job just to pay the room and board expenses and reduce the cost of future student loans. Take full advantage of everything your college has to offer you from free memberships at the campus recreational centers to give-aways at the student center. If a club or organization you are interested in is offering a pizza party as an incentive to recruit new members, there is no reason not to take advantage. If you get creative, you can even become a campus ambassador for a company that is marketing to college students and is eager to provide you their service or product for free in exchange for sharing some content via social media. In other words, manage your limited budget effectively and spend wisely. Your bank account will thank you on graduation day.

LESSON 81

BE YOURSELF

Contributed by Ashley DeSalvatore,
Rutgers University, Class of 2016

For many students in high school, it was about pretending to be someone else depending on which group you happen to be hanging out with at the time. College is a time to turn your back on who you may have been pretending to be to friends, teachers, coaches and family members and simply be yourself. The start of college is the start of an incredible journey of self-discovery. No matter how large or small the college you are attending, there is such a diverse population that by being yourself you will gravitate towards individuals with similar values, ambitions and interests. There is no need to pretend you are someone you are not. Proudly put you, your personality and your passions out there for your university community to experience and see who starts to gravitate to you.

LESSON 82

EXPLORE & EXPERIENCE

Contributed by Ashley DeSalvatore,
Rutgers University, Class of 2016

There is nothing wrong with strictly taking a numbers approach to college. For most students, they have five classes they are required to take each semester over the course of eight semesters and if they pass those 40 courses, they get to walk across the stage and receive their diploma. But college is so much more than taking 40 classes. College should be an incredible opportunity to experience and explore diverse people, places, professors, and yes, parties. If college was only about those 40 courses, students would simply take all of them online from the comfort of their home. Instead, attend athletic events and cheer on your university, participate in intramural sports, listen to a guest speaker outside the classroom setting, attend a glee club or choir concert, join a club that you never even imagined existed, sit in on a class just to learn something new without the concern of taking notes and being tested, befriend a fellow student who looks like they could use a friend. In other words, do all the things that you may have been hesitant or too embarrassed to do in high school and begin a chapter in your life that will be like no other.

LESSON 83

KNOW YOUR TIME

Contributed by Noel Fratto,
Johnson & Wales University, Class of 2018

Are you an early morning person or do you prefer nights? Do you excel when the sun rises or do you do your best thinking after noon? You can't dictate the exact time you will take your classes, but you have choices and you should understand the time of day when your mind thinks best. Of course, part-time jobs, internships, clubs and other activities influence your class schedule, but make every effort to set your class schedule around the times that are most conducive for your mental stimulation.

Author's Note: For more than five years, I have taught the same course at 8:00 a.m. every Monday and Thursday. There are students who have a challenging time waking up before noon who have had difficulties in the class. Most days they arrive late to class or don't attend at all so they quickly fall behind the course material and are always attempting to catch-up. There is a simple solution. If you excel in the afternoon, make every effort to register for courses that meet that all-important criteria. As I mention several times throughout this book, no two college students are the same and that applies to the time of day when you do your best work.

LESSON 84

SMALL MINDS TALK ABOUT PEOPLE, BIG MINDS TALK ABOUT IDEAS

Contributed by Kelsey Cuje,
Rutgers University, Class of 2017

Ignore the gossip and rumors. Avoid the petty jealousies and small talk. Instead, elevate your conversations and mind in a way that transforms not only your college experience but the experiences of those who gravitate towards you and the way you think and speak. As you take courses, especially those required in your major, you will start to recognize the students who think and act differently. They are the ones in class who engage in conversations with the professor and guest lecturers. It is these students who are living a life outside of campus. They are contributing to the local community and gaining real world experience via interesting internships and jobs. It is these students who think big and have a strategic plan and vision for life after graduation. To borrow an old adage, when it comes to college, "go big or go home." There is no room for small mindedness in the school of higher learning.

LESSON 85

ELIMINATE NEGATIVITY

Contributed by Kelsey Cuje,
Rutgers University, Class of 2017

As you settle into your freshman year, it is very easy to get caught up in negativity, complaining about your courses, professors, roommates, cafeteria food and everything else on campus that doesn't go your way. Instead, commit to a college experience that is incredibly positive. From you first day on campus, align with students who exude a positive attitude and distance yourself from those who consistently spread negativity. Every morning, wake up with a positive agenda even if you received a poor score on a test the previous day. A positive mindset and approach to your college years will result in a highly rewarding experience.

LESSON 86

DON'T FALL INTO A ROUTINE

Contributed by Ryan Rose,
Rutgers University, Class of 2017

Wake-up, go to class, eat, go to class, study and sleep late. It is very easy in college, especially freshman year, to slip into a routine of sleeping, eating and studying. Most freshmen are concerned with surviving those first 15 or 18 credits and also enjoying their new life away from mom and dad. However, you have to avoid falling into a routine. Every day, do something different - go to the campus gym, attend a unique event, listen to a guest speaker, or schedule a meeting with a professor to talk beyond the course material. In other words, do things that are not routine, not expected. By not falling into a routine, you will open yourself up to all the opportunities your campus and college have to offer and with new opportunities comes new possibilities and new people to meet.

LESSON 87

WITH FREEDOM COMES RESPONSIBILITY

Contributed by Stephen Moodie,
Rutgers University, Class of 2016

For most freshmen, it is the first time in their lives that they leave the rules of mom and dad's home for the freedom of living on their own with a few roommates. Imagine, for the first time in your life, you have no one telling you when to go to bed or when to wake-up. For the first time, no is commanding you to take out the garbage, clean up your room or eat all your vegetables. It sounds too good to be true... and it probably is. With freedom comes responsibility. In other words, the further you are from mom and dad, the greater responsibility you have. Soon after you arrive on campus and get over the initial shock of staying up all night and waking up after noon, you have to start taking responsibility and be accountable. You are not going to pass your classes unless you actually wake-up and attend them. You are not going to have a chance at earning an "A" unless you actually participate in class and spend some quality time in the library completing your required readings and studying for tests. Enjoy your first taste of freedom, but take responsibility and never forget you went to college to earn a higher education not a degree in sleeping and napping.

LESSON 88

OPEN YOURSELF UP
TO POSSIBILITIES

Contributed by Ryan Diminick,
Rutgers University, Class of 2017

Stepping onto campus is stepping into a new world of possibilities and opportunities. From challenging yourself in the classroom of higher learning to experiencing new things for the first time, go to college and open yourself up to endless possibilities. Most colleges have clubs and organizations for just about every hobby and passion point so take that first big step and join a meeting and once you enjoy that experience, visit a few more club meetings. If you enjoyed sports in high school but may not feel like you can compete at the college level, most schools offer a wide variety of sports via intramurals or club teams which offer tremendous camaraderie and an opportunity to make some immediate friends on campus. If it's the arts or music or theater that gets you excited, the possibilities are endless. All you have to do is knock on that door or take that first step into a meeting and what you may have thought was impossible becomes possible.

LESSON 89

THE REAL LESSONS ARE NOT EXPLICITLY TAUGHT

Contributed by Ryan Diminick,
Rutgers University, Class of 2017

There will be many lessons taught in class that you will be tested on and possibly soon forget once the test is completed and you are on to the next lecture or next required reading assignment. These lessons and tests play a critical role in the 40 or more individual courses you will take throughout your college career. However, there are many more valuable lessons that are not explicitly taught and which you will never be tested. These lessons may come from your professors who may offer assistance or they may come from guest lecturers who may offer real-world advice from their respective industries. Additional lessons may come from what you learn in the dorm as you experience living on your own for the first time or via your participation in a club or on a team. No matter where these real lessons originate, keep your ears and eyes open at all times, not just for that 80 minutes when you attend class, and you could walk away with learnings that you can apply for the rest of your life.

LESSON 90

EMBRACE DIVERSITY

Contributed by Austin Sommerer,
Penn State University, Class of 2017

If you embrace only one of these lessons, this is the one, especially as you start your freshman year. You are entering an incredible phase of your life where you will face a world of diversity - diverse people, backgrounds, upbringings, life experiences, perspectives and outlooks. This may be the first time in your life when you have the opportunity to witness and experience diversity on a scale this large. Don't deny or run from diversity - embrace it fully. Meet and learn from others who come from backgrounds much different than yours. Be open to engaging in diverse discussions and dialogue and let it take you to places you have never been, all while expanding your perspective in the process.

LESSON 91

SACRIFICE THE SMALL STUFF

Contributed by Ari Gutman,
Rutgers University, Class of 2017

Yes, that party on Thursday night might seem like the biggest thing in your life at the moment, but in the big picture, it is just a blip in your college career. As you experience all that college has to offer, sacrifice the small stuff. In other words, don't get caught up in small stuff - gossip, rumors, petty differences. Instead, focus on the major milestones, the big ideas, the lifelong relationships you are forming, your long-term goals and objectives. If you can keep your focus on what really matters and ignore the small stuff, your college years will be a big-time experience.

LESSON 92

FEEL AWKWARD

Contributed by Austin Sommerer,
Penn State University, Class of 2017

Feeling awkward is the key to not feeling awkward. From freshman orientation and move-in day to attending your first class and first club meeting, *everyone* feels awkward. You are not alone. Fully embrace that sense of awkwardness and go out of your way to stand out in the crowd. Make every effort to meet people, start a conversation, and engage in all the weird ice breakers and you may be surprised just how well it is received. Every other student is looking to break the ice and make new friends, but feelings of shyness, embarrassment and awkwardness sometimes prevents that. You can be the first to overcome that awkward feeling, reach out your hand, introduce yourself and make a friend for life.

LESSON 93

GETTING OUT OF YOUR COMFORT ZONE IS MANDATORY

Contributed by Austin Sommerer,
Penn State University, Class of 2017

The prior lesson discussed that feeling of awkwardness that every student experiences especially in the first semester of freshman year. That awkward feeling should force you to get out of your comfort zone. Similar to those random electives you have to take, getting out of your comfort zone is a mandatory element of your college experience. Moving away from home and moving in with strangers should make you feel uncomfortable. Embrace it and every other uncomfortable experience you come across as opposed to running away from it.

Author's Note: I will never forget my first class in college, public speaking. Within the first few minutes of class I was in front of the class sharing my life story with a room full of strangers. Was I completely uncomfortable? You bet, but that one experience was what served as my ice breaker and got me out of my comfort zone. My mindset shifted at that moment as I knew getting out of your comfort zone was exactly what I should be doing in my late teens and early 20s.

LESSON 94

COMMAND SELF-DISCIPLINE

Contributed by Samantha Franco,
Rutgers University, Class of 2018

Exercising self-discipline will be critical throughout your college career. Mom and dad will no longer be with you every step of the way telling you what to do and what not to do. It's going to be up to you to be disciplined in your approach to everything you do throughout college. From ensuring you get quality sleep to never missing classes to knowing when to leave the party and return to your dorm safely, to eating well and fueling all you have to accomplish. It will be very easy to go along with the crowd, but they may not have that same early morning class you have or a paper that is due the next day. Take accountability for yourself and your responsibilities and exercise self-discipline. It's the only way you are going to achieve those goals that you have set for yourself.

LESSON 95

OPEN YOUR MIND TO EVERYTHING

Contributed by Antonia Attardo,
Rutgers University, Class of 2019

In high school, for the most part, many of your classes and activities were set for you. In other words, you didn't need to open your mind to much because it was assigned to you. In college, you are entering an entirely new world where you can open your mind to a host of options. You don't need to accept that class schedule that every other student is taking. You can open your mind to many things in college and set your own path. If you want to study abroad for a semester, there is nothing stopping you, just like there is nothing stopping you from starting your own club or leading your classmates in a community-building effort. Consider your college years as the open era in your life and open your mind to new opportunities, experiences, relationships and possibilities.

LESSON 96

ENJOY THE MOMENT

Contributed by Reid Burch,
Loyola University Maryland, Class of 2018

Yes, your sights are set clearly on graduating and completing all the course requirements before you, but your college experience is comprised of a series of incredible moments that you may never experience again. Take the time to enjoy these moments, whether it's celebrating the school's upset football victory over your rival or the time your group aces the final class presentation and receives accolades from the professor. Don't just move ahead to the next thing on your to-do list. Instead, stop, and savor the moment. These moments may come regularly - making your first college friend, attending your first club meeting, becoming a member of a sports team and the camaraderie that comes with it. Don't just shrug these moments off. They are part of your unique college experience and should be celebrated. Four years goes by very fast. Hit the pause button every once in a while and just take a moment to look around, pat yourself on the back and enjoy your current life stage as a flourishing college student.

LESSON 97

TRY SOMETHING NEW

Contributed by Caroline Petrone,
University of South Carolina, Class of 2017

As a teen-ager, you enjoyed a series of new experiences each and every year - first job, first time driving and first time leaving mom and dad and living on your own at college. Don't stop trying new things when you get to college. Open yourself up to new people, opportunities and experiences. If you fully leverage your college experience, you should be trying something new on almost a daily basis - meet a classmate, listen to a guest speaker, support a charitable community event, sit in on a course you aren't registered for to learn if you may want to take it the following semester, request a meeting with your professor and join a club. Those are just a few of the new things you can do almost any day in college and the list is endless. It is up to you to take the first step, be an explorer and seek out something new every day.

LESSON 98

DON'T HESITATE

Contributed by Daijie Yuan,
Rutgers University, Class of 2017

Your college years will pass by quicker than you can imagine so don't hesitate to get fully involved. In other words, don't put off to tomorrow what you can do today. From your first week on campus, don't hesitate to make new friends, introduce yourself to your professor, join a club, participate in intramurals, cheer on your school's sports teams and so much more. There are an endless amount of opportunities and possibilities on your campus so don't hesitate to take full advantage.

LESSON 99

MAKE MISTAKES

Contributed by Daijie Yuan,
Rutgers University, Class of 2017

Your college years should be comprised of a series of "test and learn" experiences. College offers you an open invitation to try things, make mistakes and then apply those learnings to future efforts. While in college, don't run away from mistakes and failed attempts - embrace them. While earning an "A" in your classes may be a primary objective, don't have the mindset that you can't fail at something. Whether in or outside the classroom, make mistakes and learn from those mistakes. You will be able to file away what you learned and apply it to a future experience in college or many years down the road in your career.

LESSON 100

DECLARE YOUR INDEPENDENCE

Contributed by Zahra Abbasi,
Rutgers University, Class of 2016

Whether you move cross-country to attend college or commute every day to a campus just down the road from your parent's home, you are entering an age of independence, unlike anything you have experienced in your lifetime. Declare your independence and embrace this opportunity to make decisions on your own. From simple day-to-day decisions like deciding if you are going to wake up and attend class to much more significant decisions like declaring your major and creating a successful path to your future career, you now have the independence to decide your next move. Your parents and others will always be around to provide support and assistance, but fully embrace this new age of independence and individual responsibility.

LESSON 101

LIKE SUCCESS, COLLEGE IS A MARATHON

Contributed by Alec Prieto,
Rutgers University Class of 2018

While four years flies by fast and you will be walking across the stage receiving your diploma before you know it, your college experience will be a marathon featuring many highs and lows and starts and stops. You will face more anxiety and indecision in the first semester of your freshman year than you will the next three years combined. As the expression goes, "never let your emotions get too high or too low." You will make friends and you will lose friends. You will have your heart broken and your heart pumping with incredible energy and excitement. You will have professors who you gel with seamlessly and others who you think never even knew your name. You will make incredible memories that will last forever and a few regrets that you hope don't last past the weekend. Your college experience is everything you make of it and everything that you put into it. This marathon we call college is a two-way street and the more you take charge of your unique college experience with a proactive mindset and an immersive "two-feet in" approach, the more your college or university will reward you with an endless number of moments and lessons that you can leverage for a lifetime.

FINAL THOUGHTS

I hope that these 101 lessons contributed by current college students and recent graduates from across the country will help make your transition from high school to college as seamless as possible. When I stepped on the campus at Rutgers University as a freshman in 1985, there was no book that provided valuable insights and recommendations from those students who had previously enjoyed the college experience and all the challenges and opportunities that came with it. I am inspired each and every day by the university students I teach and mentor and I hope the lessons that those students have contributed in this book inspire you as you set out on your own unique college journey and that one day, you will share with the next generation of college students your own learnings. Congratulations on graduating high school and best wishes for a very successful college experience!

ABOUT THE AUTHOR

Since 2013, Mark Beal has served as an adjunct professor in the School of Communication at Rutgers University in New Brunswick, New Jersey. He has designed and taught 300 and 400 level courses including Media, Marketing and Communication; Leadership in Groups & Organizations; Principles of Public Relations; and Message Design for Public Relations. During that time, he has taught more than 1,000 students and mentored many more across the nation. It was these students who inspired Mark to write his first book, *101 Lessons They Never Taught You In College*, which was published in 2017 and is available for purchase on Amazon. The book serves as a guide for students as they navigate the transition from college to a career.

Mark brings his 101 lessons to life via his podcast series, *101 Lessons in Leadership*. In each podcast episode, Mark interviews a leader and delves into the mentors who inspired them as well as the lessons in leadership and life that they share with their current followers. The podcast episodes can be listened to for free by simply going to www.101lessonspodcast.com.

Aside from teaching, Mark has developed and executed award-winning public relations and marketing campaigns for some of the most recognizable brands for the past 25 years. His marketing work has taken him to the Olympic Games, Super Bowl, World Series, US Open and "on tour" with The Rolling Stones.

Mark received his BA in journalism from Rutgers University and his MA in communications from Kent State University. He lives in Toms River, NJ with his wife, Michele, where they enjoy boating paddle boarding, cycling, running, swimming, tennis and golf. They have three children, Drew, Meghan, Summer, a daughter-in-law, Huda, and two grandchildren, Luke and Marc.

Twitter: @markbealpr
Email: markbeal@markbealmedia.com
Phone: +1.848.992.0391

Made in the
USA
Middletown, DE